FUNNY MAGIC

Easy Tricks for Young Magicians

by Rose Wyler & Gerald Ames

Pictures by Tālivaldis Stubis

PARENTS' MAGAZINE PRESS/NEW YORK

Library of Congress Cataloging in Publication Data

Wyler, Rose, 1909-
    Funny magic.
    SUMMARY: Directions for performing a variety of
simple magic tricks.

    1. Conjuring—Juvenile literature. [1. Magic
tricks] I. Ames, Gerald, 1906-   joint author.
II. Stubis, Talivaldis, illus. III. Title.
GV1548.W84   793.8   73-39866
ISBN 0-8193-0584-7
ISBN 0-8193-0585-5 (lib. bdg.)

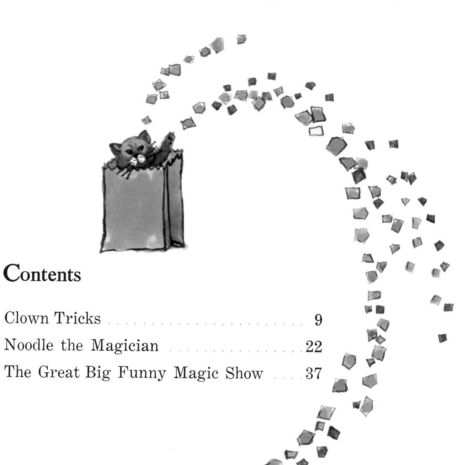

Contents

CLOWN TRICKS

Look at you, all dressed up
in clothes that are too big
and a hat that's too small.
Hi, clown!
Hi, funny face!
Your big red nose is a fake.
It's just a rubber ball,
cut to fit over your real nose.
People will laugh at you
and your tricks because
the tricks will be funny.
And to make sure they work,
try them first
in front of a mirror.

Are you ready, clown?

Blow up a balloon by magic

Here is your first clown trick.

You are looking for something.

You look high and low.

You look into a paper bag on the table.

You turn the bag upside down.

A red balloon falls out.

There! You found what you wanted.

You let the air out of the balloon

and drop the empty balloon into the bag.

Then you bend over the bag and

blow,
    blow,
        blow.

You look into the bag.

You reach into it and pull out—

the balloon, blown up big and round.

The trick:
Use two red balloons.
Blow them up.
Stick one in the bag with sticky tape.
Drop the other balloon in on top.
No one will know there are two balloons
in the bag.

Balance a hair

Pretend to pull a hair
from your head.
Hold the make-believe hair
between your finger and thumb.
Turn your face up.
Pretend to stand the hair
on your big clown nose.
Take your hand away.
Careful now!
Move your head this way and that.
There! You are balancing the hair.
Now carefully take it off your nose.
How clever you are!
You wave and make a bow.

Lift a card with a hair

Hold up the make-believe hair
between your finger and thumb.
With your other hand,
hold up a pack of cards.
Now pretend to stick the end
of the make-believe hair
onto the card nearest you.
Slowly pull the hair up and—
the card slowly rises.

The trick:
Your thumb is on the nearest card.
You push the card up
with your thumb.

Smell a color

Your friend Tom holds up a box of crayons.

You sniff at it.

Tom says, "The clown thinks

he can smell colors.

Let's give him a test."

Tom turns you around

so you can't see what he does.

He takes all the crayons out of the box.

He chooses one—say it is red—

and puts it back in the box.

He tells you to hold your hands

behind your back.

He puts the box in your hands.

Now for the test!

You hold the box to your nose

and sniff at it.

Tom asks, "Is the crayon blue?"

You shake your head.

"Is it yellow?" You shake your head.

"Is it red?"

You bob your head up and down,

yes, yes, yes!

When Tom gives you tests with other colors,

you smell the color every time.

The trick:

You are always right because you see the color.

When the box is behind you,

you stick your thumb in

and scratch the crayon with your thumbnail.

When you hold the box to your nose,

you look at the color on your thumbnail.

The loose thread

You hold up your hand
to shade your eyes.
You look and look.
Who is that—
your old friend Joe!
You shake his hand.
You slap him on the back.
You hug him.
Then you stare at his shirt
and shake your head.
There is a loose thread on his shirt.
You take hold of the thread.
You pull it. You pull and pull.
The thread comes out and out.
It reaches across the room.
You hand the end to someone else.
The thread keeps coming out, endlessly.

The trick:
You and Joe get ready together.
Use a spool of thread.
Thread a needle with it.
Put the spool inside Joe's shirt.
Run the thread out through his shirt.
Then take off the needle
and let the thread hang loose.

Balance a glass

Can a glass be balanced
on the edge of a plate?
A good clown can do it.
Your friends are pop-eyed
when you show them.

The trick:
From behind, it looks like this.
Your thumb is under the glass,
and holds it up.

Push a knife through the glass

Now hold up the glass, upside down.
Take a table knife and push it up
into the glass.
Pretend you want to make it go
through the bottom.
You try. *Click!*
The knife hits the bottom of the glass.
You push it up again.
The knife does not go through.
You make a face.
You try again.
There! the knife goes right up
through the glass.

The trick:
The last time you push up the knife,
you slide it behind *the glass.*
It seems to go through the bottom.

How to fix a watch

Look at your wrist
and shake your head.
No watch!
What time is it?
Borrow a watch from Suzy.
Hold it in your left hand.
Look at it.
Put the watch to your ear,
then shake your head.
Something is wrong with the watch.
Well, you will fix it.
Pass the watch to your right hand.
Raise your right hand high—
dash the watch to the floor.
Crash! Good-bye watch!
Then pick up the pieces.
Surprise! The pieces are only nails.

The trick:
Just pretend to pass the watch
to your right hand,
but really keep it in your left hand.
Have the nails ready in your right hand.

NOODLE THE MAGICIAN

Meet Noodle.

He's only a puppet
but he can do magic tricks.
Noodle is a hand puppet.
His face is made of paper,
taped onto a handkerchief.
To hold the puppet,
put your hand under the handkerchief.
Move your hand and
Noodle will nod his head, yes,
or shake his head, no.
Your thumb and a finger are his hands.
And is he clever with his hands!
He can even pick up a pencil
and use it as a magic wand.
Put the handkerchief over a pop bottle
and Noodle will stand all by himself.

Surprise from a hat

A hat lies on the table.
What is under it?
Have Noodle pick up the hat.
There is nothing under it.
Noodle turns the hat over
and puts it back on the table.
Noodle waves his wand over the hat.
Then he reaches into it and pulls out—
a long ribbon.

The trick:
Use a roll of paper ribbon.
Put the roll under the band inside the hat.
It will stay there
when the hat is right side up.
When the hat is turned over,
the roll of ribbon slips down.
Then Noodle can take hold of the end
and pull the ribbon out.

The rabbit gets away

You say, "Can you pull anything else
out of the empty hat?"
Noodle nods, yes.
"What? A rabbit?"
Again Noodle nods.
Noodle picks up the hat
and shows the inside.
There is nothing in it.
He puts the hat down,
reaches into it,
and shakes his head.
"What's the matter, Noodle?
Did the rabbit get away?"
The puppet nods, yes.
"Too bad!"
Then Noodle *does* pull something
out of the hat—a carrot!
"What do you know!" you say.
"That's the carrot the rabbit was eating."

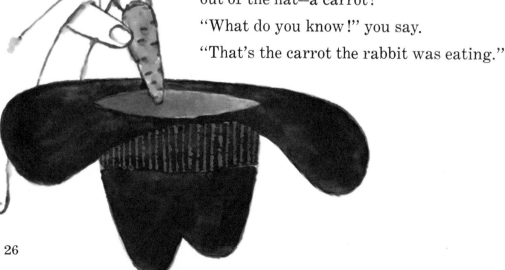

The trick:

Have the carrot ready on your lap.

When Noodle reaches into the hat,

drop the carrot in with your other hand.

Do this behind the puppet,

so nobody sees it.

Drop a penny through a plate

Say, "Noodle's next trick is with a penny."
Wrap the penny in a piece of paper,
put it on a small plate,
and set the plate on a glass.
Pick up the puppet.
Give him his magic wand.
He waves it over the plate,
then taps the plate.
He taps until—*clink*—
the penny falls into the glass.
It drops right through the plate!

Does it really?
Shake out the paper.
Yes, it's empty.

The trick:

Rub some soap on the bottom of the plate.

Then press a penny against the plate

and make it stick.

Nobody knows about this *penny.*

But what about the other one?

You only pretend to wrap it in the paper.

You really let that penny slip out

and fall into your lap.

When Noodle taps the plate,

push the plate a little.

The penny that is stuck on it

rubs against the rim of the glass.

It comes loose and falls into the glass.

The tame bee

You hold out your hand and show
a wad of paper shaped like a bee.
You say, "This is Noodle's tame bee.
His name is Bumble.
Bumble doesn't sting—
do you Bumble?
B-z-z-z.
Bumble says no."

Bumble's house is on the table.

It's a paper cup, standing upside down.

You set Bumble on the cup

so Noodle can see him.

Pretend to take the bee in your hand.

Say to Bumble,

"Do you want to fly around a little?"

You open your hand—it's empty.

You look up in the air.

Noodle looks, too.

"There goes Bumble," you say.

"*Bz-z-z-z-z-z-z-z-z.*"

"Now, Bumble, come back home.
Go into your house."
Noodle lifts the edge of the cup a little
so the bee can get under it.
Pick up the cup and—there is the bee!

The trick:
Half the bottom is cut out of the cup.
This doesn't show when you do the trick.
People sitting in front of you
just see the side of the cup.
When you pretend to catch the bee,
push it into the hole.

Noodle's cookies

You open a magazine and turn some pages.
Show Noodle the magazine and say,
"Here is a good recipe.
It tells how to make magic cookies.
Do you want to make some?"
The puppet nods.

You read what goes into the cookies—
"Two pickles,
one chopped-up mitten,
a dab of shoe polish.
For magic cookies you don't need an oven.
Mix things right in the magazine."
Noodle just pretends to toss each thing
into the magazine.

You shake the magazine and—
out come some *real* cookies.
Good for Noodle!

The trick:
Get the magazine ready this way.
Paste two pages together at the bottom.
This makes a pocket.
Put some cookies into it.
The cookies stay there
while you read the recipe.
They fall out when you hold the magazine
upside down and shake it.

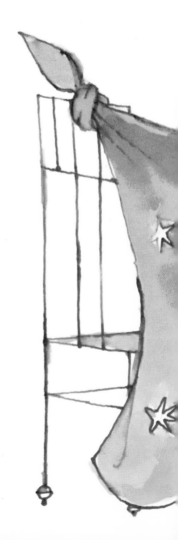

THE GREAT BIG FUNNY MAGIC SHOW

Here are some more good tricks.
For some of them
you need a helper or two.
Work on them together.
Then, when you are ready,
call in your friends to see—
The Great Big Funny Magic Show.
How will it begin?
Maybe with a funny song.

The upside-down singer

The stage is set.
The curtain is a sheet
stretched between two chairs.
You say, "And now, my friends,
we bring you—The Great Singer, Billy.
Give him a hand, everybody."
Clap-clap.
Billy sings a song.
Then you say, "Billy is so good,
he can sing standing on his head."
Billy's head goes down,
and his feet come up behind the curtain.
He sings even better than before.

Then you have an "accident."
You knock down the curtain.
And there on the floor sits Billy,
holding up his shoes.

Billy loses his shirt

Have Billy sit on a chair.
You look him over.
You stare at his shirt collar and say,
"That shirt is terrible."
Take hold of Billy's shirt collar,
give it a pull and—
off comes his shirt,
but not his jacket!

The trick:
When Billy puts his shirt on,
he does not put his arms into the sleeves.
The sleeves hang down loose.
He puts on his jacket,
and the loose shirt sleeves
don't show.

Smash hit

Billy is mad—real mad.
He takes something out of his pocket—
an egg.
He aims it at you.
You duck but—
Plop! The egg hits you and breaks.
And out of it comes—
paper confetti!

The trick:
Ask a grown-up to help you
get the egg ready.
Use scissors to jab a small hole
in one end of the shell.
Cut away the shell around the hole
and make the hole as big as a dime.
Then jab the skin under the shell.
Shake the egg out of the shell
and give it to your mother for cooking.
Wash out the empty shell
and set it aside to dry.
For confetti,
cut up a page from a magazine.
Fill the shell with confetti.
Stick tape over the hole and
the egg is ready for a smash hit.

Handkerchief from nowhere

Say, "What do I have in my hands?
Nothing.
Or do I have something in them?
I can never be sure.
Sometimes I surprise myself."
Pull back your sleeves.
Nothing is hidden in them.
Then hold out your hands.
Rub them together.
As you rub your hands,
a handkerchief begins to appear
between your fingers.
Shake it out and show it around.

The trick:

Use a small handkerchief.

Squeeze it into a ball.

Hide it in the bend of your left arm.

Pull back your right sleeve first.

As you pull back the left sleeve,

take the handkerchief from your arm.

Cut a string, then make it whole

Hold up a long string.
Double it to make a loop.
Move the loop to your left hand and
let the ends hang loose.
Pull up the loop a little.
Ask Sally to take scissors and
cut off the loop.
She cuts it off.

You say, "Now the string is cut in two."
Make passes with your hand.
"Abracadabra! Abracadabra!
String, become whole again.
Now, Sally, pull out the string."
Sally pulls it out and—
the string is whole!

The trick:
Use two strings—one long, one short.
When you start the trick,
the short string is looped
and hidden in your left hand.
You pull up this string to be cut.
The loop of the long string
is also in your left hand,
but no one sees it.

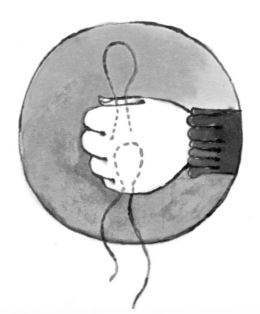

The pet egg

For this trick use a hard-boiled egg.
Tie a string around it and
pull the egg, like a dog on a leash.
Then take off the string.
Say, "This little egg is my pet.
It does what I tell it to do.
Don't you, Little Egg?"
Two paper cups and two handkerchiefs
are on the table before you.
Set one cup in your left hand,
drop in the egg,
and cover the cup with a handkerchief.

Then put the cup on the table and say,
"Stay there a while, Little Egg."
Turn the other cup upside down
to show it is empty.
Turn it right side up again,
and set it on your left hand.
Cover it with the other handkerchief.
Then look at the cup on the table.
Talk to the egg.
Say, "Now, Little Egg, come here.
Get into the cup in my hand."
Flip off the handkerchief,
turn the cup over in your right hand and—
there is Little Egg!

The trick:
Cut the bottom out of each cup.
When you do the trick,
people are sitting in front of you,
and they can't see the cut-out bottoms.
They see only the sides of the cups.
When you take the first cup from your hand
and set it on the table,
the egg stays in your hand.
When you set the other cup on your hand,
it goes right over the egg.

X-ray eyes

Say, "And now for the greatest trick of all.
I'll show you that I have X-ray eyes.
I can see what's on a paper
even if the paper is covered.
Who wants to write something?"
Joan says she will.
She writes on the paper.
Tell her to fold the paper,
put it on the floor,
and stand on it.
Joan does. Then she says,
"O.K. What's on the paper?"
"That's easy," you say. "Your big feet."

But what *did* Joan write on the paper?

Hold up the paper so everyone can read: